Front Porch
Old-Time Songs
Jokes & Stories

48 Great Sing-Along Favorites

by
Wayne Erbsen

Order No. FPS-100   Native Ground Music   ISBN 0-9629327-9-5

Contents

Courtesy of Jim Bollman Collection

Places Everyone!

Quickly now...take your seats. The first day of music class is about to begin. A hush falls over the classroom as the Professor enters the room and takes the podium. The words that come out of the mustached and bespectacled professor's mouth will surprise, amaze and jolt even those students trying to catch a cat nap in the back row.

You *DON'T* have to have a good voice to sing any of the songs in *Front Porch Old-Time Songs, Jokes & Stories*. You don't need to know how to read music or even play an instrument. Nor do you need "ear training," voice lessons, experience with a choir, or a note from your grammar school music teacher. To sing out of this book, you can be deaf in one ear and can't hear out of the other. You can possess what we refer to in the music business as "tin ear."

Perhaps in the past you have been embarrassed to sing. Maybe people have cracked rude jokes when you attempted to carry a tune and you have felt humiliated, humbled, even mortified. You may actually prefer reading your *Front Porch Old-Time Songs, Jokes & Stories* in the closet, so even your family doesn't know that deep within your bosom, you harbor the longing to explode in song.

Courtesy of Jim Bollman Collection

It's time to come out of the closet! As a Professor of Old Time Music, I assure you that the songs you'll find in these pages have traditionally been sung by people with "bad" voices. In fact, they sound *better* that way. Can you imagine someone singing *Bile Em Cabbages Down* with an operatic voice? I can't think of anything more ridiculous! Can you??

So take the advice of one old-timer and sing by the "letter method." Just take a deep breath, open your mouth, and 'let 'er fly!'

Class dismissed.

Old Time Songs

The style we refer to as "Old Time Music" is actually composed of almost a dozen types of songs. Before you begin singing your way through *Front Porch Old-Time Songs, Jokes & Stories*, you might like to know in which category some of your favorite songs fall.

Animal Songs: Cluck Old Hen, The Crawdad Song, Ground Hog.

Civil War Songs: Goober Peas, When Johnny Comes Marching Home, Yellow Rose of Texas

Fiddle Tunes: Arkansas Traveler, Soldier's Joy, Uncle Joe.

Gospel: Amazing Grace, Poor Wayfaring Stranger, Unclouded Day.

Love Songs: Down in the Valley, My Home's Across the Smoky Mountains, On Top of Old Smoky, The Riddle Song, When You And I Were Young, Maggie, Wildwood Flower.

Minstrel Songs: Bile Em Cabbage Down, Blue Tail Fly, Buffalo Gals, Oh! Susanna, Oh, Them Golden Slippers, Polly Wally Doodle, Turkey in the Straw.

Murder Ballads: Poor Ellen Smith, Pretty Polly.

Sentimental Songs: Grandfather's Clock, Home Sweet Home, Listen to the Mockingbird, My Old Kentucky Home.

Songs of Rascals, Ornery Cusses, and Wild Women: Cindy, Jack of Diamonds, Jesse James, John Henry, Moonshiner, Old Dan Tucker, Old Joe Clark, Roving Gambler, Wild Bill Jones.

Songs That Defy Categories: Hambone.

Train Songs: New River Train, Railroad Bill, Wabash Cannonball.

Singing With or Without an Instrument

In order to fully get your two cents worth out of this book, here are a few secrets or tricks. If you're singing the songs *without* accompaniment, and you're familiar with the tune, just jump in and sing it; you don't need to know a lick about music.

If you play a few chords on the guitar and want to strum along as you sing, the chords are written over the music in each song. If you have a guitar, but can't play it, the guitar chords are provided for you at the end of the book. *Hint:* When making a chord, *always* make the fingers of your left hand plunk down on the chord all-at-the-same-time. This is essential for learning to change chords quickly.

Courtesy of Jim Bollman Collection

The chords in a particular song make up a little family called a "key." You can always tell what key a song is in by looking at the **last** chord of the song. If a song ends with a G chord, you can be sure it's in the key of G. The keys were chosen to suit the vocal range of the average male voice with a *normal* range. If you are not *normal* or male, you may want to consult this handy guide to choosing a key.

Average Male Voice:	Key of G A C D E
Average Female	*is equal to*
(or High Male Voice):	Key of C D F G A

In so many words, if a song is pitched in the key of G, for example, a female or a male with a high voice would most likely sing it in the key of C. This is not an absolute rule, only a place to start searching for the right key to sing it in.

Changing Keys

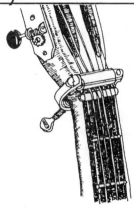

I f a song is too high or too low for your voice, don't hesitate to change the key. The easiest way to do it is by using a capo. A capo is nothing more than a glorified pencil and rubber band. Simply apply the capo to the second, third, or fourth fret of your guitar or banjo until the song is more comfortable to sing. (Don't try a capo on a piano or xylophone.)

Another way to change keys is to simply pick another family of chords to play in. If a song is too low, simply go *up* the alphabet a letter or two until it sings right. If A is too low, go to C or D or...If a song is too high, simply go *down* the alphabet from D to C or A.

John Edwards Memorial Foundation

Besides having names like G and A, chords also have numbers. Most of the songs in this book have just three chords: I, IV, and V. To change keys, simply select a new key, and substitute the new chords for the old ones, as shown on the diagram below.

Harvey & Leonard Copeland

Key of	I	IV	V
A	A	D	E
C	C	F	G
D	D	G	A
E	E	A	B
F	F	B♭	C
G	G	C	D

Amazing Grace

The life of John Newton, the composer of *Amazing Grace*, reads like it was torn from the pages of a fiction writer like Robert Louis Stevenson....Born in 1725, he went to sea at the age of nine after becoming an orphan. Captured after deserting from the British navy, he was put in irons and publicly whipped. He then signed on with a slave ship which carried its human cargo from Africa to America.

When Newton was twenty-three, his ship was battered by a violent storm. Thinking the vessel would go down, he turned to God. Although he eventually became captain of a slave ship, he continued to study the Bible. At the age of thirty-nine he gave up life on the sea and was ordained as a minister of the Church of England. Legends tell that even as a pastor of the church in Olney, England, he continued to wear the uniform of a sea captain while toting a cane in one hand and a Bible in the other. It was in Olney where Newton composed *Amazing Grace*, setting the words to an anonymous hymn tune. It often appears in old hymn books under the title "New Britain" or "Harmony Grove." It remains the best known hymn in America.

Chorus A - ma - zing grace how sweet the sound that saved a wretch like me. I once was lost but now I'm found was blind but now I see.

'Twas grace that taught my heart to fear
And grace my fears relieved
How precious did that grace appear
The hour I first believed

Through many dangers, toils and snares
I have already come
'Twas grace that brought me safe thus far
And grace will lead me home

When we've been there ten thousand years
Bright shining as the sun
We've no less days to sing God's praise
Than when we first begun

Arkansas Traveler

Arkansas Traveler is the famous fiddle tune that comes complete with its own skit. The tune was first printed on February 23, 1847 and the dialog is generally credited to Colonel Sandford C. Faulkner, who became known as "The Arkansas Traveler". A farmer was playing the fiddle on his front porch in rural Arkansas when up rides a stranger. The following conversation is said to have taken place.

Stranger: Does this road go to Little Rock?
Farmer: I've lived here 20 years and it ain't gone nowhere yet!
Stranger: Does it make any difference which one of these roads I take? **Farmer:** Not to me.
Stranger: Is that creek over there fordable? **Farmer:** The ducks cross it every day.
Stranger: But how deep's the water? **Farmer:** It comes up to "here" on the ducks.
Stranger: Can't you tell me how deep it is? **Farmer:** There's water all the way to the bottom.
Stranger: Does the wind blow this-a way all the time?
Farmer: No, sometimes it blows the other way.
Stranger: Your corn's awful little and yellow. **Farmer:** We planted the little yellow kind.
Stranger: How'd your taters turn out?
Farmer: They didn't turn out; me and Sal dug them out!
Stranger: I noticed your wife's dress is mighty short.
Farmer: It'll be long enough before she gets another one.
Stranger: How long have you lived here?
Farmer: See that mountain over there? It was here when I arrived.
Stranger: Have you lived here all your life? **Farmer:** Not yet.
Stranger: How far did you go in school? **Farmer:** About ten miles.
Stranger: No, I mean what grade? **Farmer:** Pretty steep.
Stranger: I noticed it's raining and your roof leaks. Why don't you fix it?
Farmer: When it's raining I can't, and when it's not, it don't leak.
Stranger: You don't know much. **Farmer:** Nope, but I'm not lost.
Stranger: Well, you're not very far from a fool.
Farmer: Just these steps between us.
Stranger: Why don't you play the second part of that tune?
Farmer: I don't know it. Can you play it? **Stranger:** Why sure I can!
Farmer: In that case, why don't you stay for supper?

Bile Em Cabbage Down

*B*ile Em Cabbage Down is a minstrel tune from the 1850's. The verses float from song to song and can be found in *Shady Grove, Whoa Mule,* and *Lynchburg Town,* among others. The "hoe cakes" described in the song were a favorite in the antebellum South. Slaves apparently cooked hoe cakes on their hoes over an open fire. Confederate soldiers reportedly roasted them on bayonets.

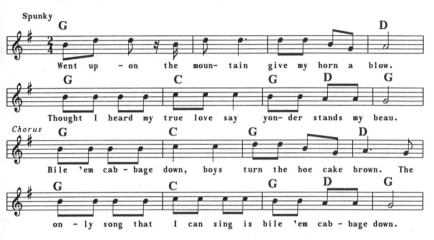

Spunky
Went up-on the moun-tain give my horn a blow.
Thought I heard my true love say yon-der stands my beau.

Chorus
Bile 'em cab-bage down, boys turn the hoe cake brown. The
on-ly song that I can sing is bile 'em cab-bage down.

Went to see my gal last night
I done it kind a-sneakin'
Kissed her mouth and hit her nose,
And the doggone thing was leakin'

Raccoon up a 'simmon tree
Possum on the ground
Raccoon said to the possum
Shake them 'simmons down

Jaybird died with the whooping cough
Sparrow died with the colic
Along come the frog with a fiddle on his back
Inquirin' his way to the frolic

Took my gal to the blacksmith shop
To have her mouth made small
She turned around a time or two
And swallowed the shop and all

Uncle Dave Macon

*"It ain't what you got,
it's what you put out."*

-Uncle Dave Macon

Courtesy of Charles K. Wolfe

9

Blue-Tail Fly

Suited up in black-face and wearing a baggy tuxedo, his friends liked to call him "Uncle Dan." But it was Daniel Emmett's song about the lowly fly that really got people buzzing. First published in about 1846, The *Blue Tail Fly* became a national hit, bumping along in covered wagons to the California gold rush and riding in grand style down the Mississippi River on a riverboat. President Lincoln called it "that buzzing song" and is said to have played it on his harmonica.

When I was young I used to wait On master and serve him his plate And pass the bottle when he got dry, And brush a-way the blue tail fly. Jim-my crack corn and I don't care. Jim-my crack corn and I don't care. Jim-my crack corn and I don't care. My mas-ter's gone a-way.

Then after dinner he would sleep
A vigil I would have to keep
And when he wanted to shut his eye
He told me, "Watch the blue-tail fly"

One day he rode around the farm
The flies so numerous, they did swarm
One chanced to bite him on the thigh
The devil take the blue-tail fly

The pony run, he jump and pitch
And tumble master in the ditch
He died, the jury they wondered why
The verdict was the blue-tail fly

They laid him 'neath a 'simmon tree
His epitaph is there to see:
"Beneath this stone I'm forced to lie
A victim of the blue-tail fly"

Ol' master's gone, now let him rest
They say that things are for the best
I can't forget till the day I die
Ol' master and the blue-tail fly

Buffalo Gals

Changing names seems to be a habit with *Buffalo Gals*. Even its composer changed his name from John Hodges to Cool White. *Buffalo Gals* started out in 1844 as *Lubbly Fan*, but its name soon changed with each touring minstrel troupe which took it on the road (Bowry Gals, Cincinatti Gals, Lousiana Gals, Charleston Gals, etc). By 1848 the name *Buffalo Gals* stuck, but even into the 1920's groups like The Skillet Lickers called it *Alabama Gals*.

As I was lumb-ring down the street Down the street down the street. A
hand-some gal I chanced to meet. Oh, she was fair to view.

Chorus
Buf - fa - lo gals won't ya come out to - night.
Come out to - night come out to - night.
Buf - fa - lo gals won't ya come out to- night. We'll
dance by the light of the moon.

I asked her if she'd have talk
Have a talk, have a talk
Her feet took up the whole sidewalk
As she stood close to me

I asked her, "Would you want to dance
Want to dance, want to dance?"
I thought that I would have a chance
To shake a foot with her

Oh, I danced with the gal with a hole in her stockin'
And her hip kept a-rockin' and her toe kept a-knockin'
I danced with the gal with a hole in her stockin'
And we danced by the light of the moon

11

Cindy

Cindy, the story of a spunky and mischievous gal, has been a favorite since its origins in the minstrel days before the Civil War. The old gal is still up to her old tricks, because she constantly borrows verses from other songs, while the chorus stays pretty much hers. *Cindy* was first recorded by Samantha Bumgardner and Eva Davis from Western North Carolina for Columbia Records in 1924, making them the first women in country music to be recorded.

You ought to see my Cindy. She lives a way down South. She's so sweet the hon-ey bees swarm a-round her mouth. Get a-long home, Cin-dy, Cin-dy, Get a-long home, Cin-dy, Cin-dy, Get a-long home, Cin-dy, Cin-dy, I'll mar-ry you some day.

Cindy in the summer time,
Cindy in the fall
If I can't get Cindy all the time
I won't have her at all

I wish I was an apple
A-hanging on a tree
Every time that Cindy passed
She'd take a bite of me

I took my Cindy to preaching
And what do you reckon she done?
She stood right up in the preacher's face
And chewed her chewing gum

Cindy got to preaching
She shouted all around
She got so full of glory
She rolled her stockings down

When I go a-fishing
I go with a hook and line
And when I go to marry
I go with a willing mind

Where'd you get your whiskey?
Where'd you get your dram?
Where'd you get your whiskey?
Way down in Rockingham

Cindy got religion
She got it once before
But when she hears my old banjo
She's the first one on the floor!

I went to see Miss Cindy
I hadn't been there before
She fed me in the chicken coop,
And I ain't going there no more

Cluck Old Hen

While modern country singers seem to like to sing about pick-up trucks, trains, mothers and jails, old time musicians often found the chicken to be a worthy subject of numerous songs. (*Cacklin Hen, Chicken Reel, Rise When the Rooster Crows, Chicken Don't Roost Too High For Me* and *C-H-I-C-K-E-N).*

Romping

| D | C | D | G | D |

My old   hen's   a   good ole   hen,   She   lays   eggs for the
Some- times eight,   some-times ten,   That's e - nough for the

A7   D   *Chorus* D   C

rail - road   men.   Cluck   old   hen,   cluck   and   sing,
rail - road   men.   Cluck   old   hen,   cluck   and   squall,

D   A7   D

Ain't   laid   an   egg   since   way___   last   spring.
Ain't   laid   an   egg   since   way___   last   fall.

Library of Congress

My old hen, she won't do
She lays eggs and taters too
First time she cackled, she cackled in the lot
Next time she cackled, she cackled in the pot

I had a little hen, she had a wooden leg
Best darn hen that ever laid an egg
Laid more eggs than any hen around the barn
Another little drink wouldn't do me any harm

Cluck old hen, cluck and tell you
If you don't cluck, I'm gonna sell you
The old hen cackled, she cackled for corn
The old hen cackled when the chicken's all gone

What did the surprised hen say after laying a square egg‽

☛ *Ouch!!!* [1]

The Crawdad Song

L egends tell us that when French settlers were expelled from the Acadian peninsula in Canada by the British, they journeyed to Louisiana. Along the way, they were followed by schools of lobsters who nearly starved to death and turned into tiny crawfish. Following the example of the 'Cadians (Cajuns) who build homes with tall chimneys, the crayfish built chimneys out of mud.

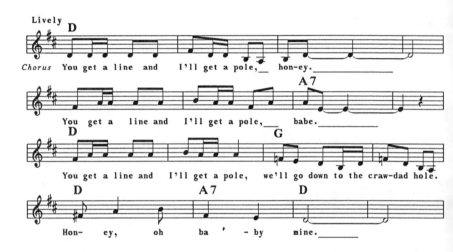

Chorus: You get a line and I'll get a pole, hon-ey.
You get a line and I'll get a pole, babe.
You get a line and I'll get a pole, we'll go down to the craw-dad hole.
Hon-ey, oh ba'-by mine.

Yonder stands a man with a pack on his back, honey
Yonder stands a man with a pack on his back, babe
Yonder stands a man with a pack on his back
Got all the crawdads he can pack
Honey, oh baby mine

What you gonna do when the lake runs dry, baby
What you gonna do when the lake runs dry, babe
What you gonna do when the lake runs dry
Sit on the banks and watch the crawdads die
Honey, oh baby mine

Wake up now you slept too late, honey
Wake up now you slept too late, babe
Wake up now you slept too late
Crawdad man done passed your gate
Honey, oh baby mine

Cripple Creek

Both North Carolina and Colorado claim to have originated the tune *Cripple Creek*. Bascomb Lamar Lunsford, an early collector of mountain music, wrote on April 2, 1929 that *Cripple Creek* "takes its name from a wild mountain stream near Asheville, NC." He added that, "these lines have been written within a five minute walk of Cripple Creek." If we can believe Lunsford, who lived near Asheville, the real Cripple Creek has been found!

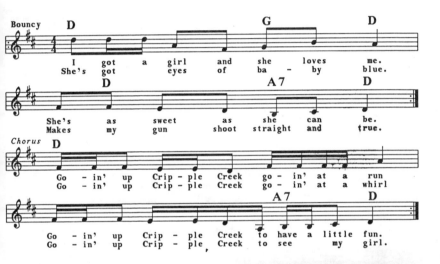

I got a girl and she loves me.
She's got eyes of ba - by blue.

She's as sweet as she can be.
Makes my gun shoot straight and true.

Chorus

Go - in' up Crip - ple Creek go - in' at a run
Go - in' up Crip - ple Creek go - in' at a whirl

Go - in' up Crip - ple Creek to have a little fun.
Go - in' up Crip - ple, Creek to see my girl.

Cripple Creek's wide and Cripple Creek's deep,
I'll wade old Cripple Creek before I sleep
Roll my britches to my knees,
I wade old Cripple Creek when I please

I went down to Cripple Creek
To see what them girls had to eat
I got drunk and fell against the wall
Ole corn liquor was the cause of it all

> "Doctor, will I be able to play the banjo after surgery?" "Absolutely." "That's great, 'cause I was never able to play one before!" [2]

Courtesy of Jim Bollman Collection

15

Down in the Valley

ountry people have always loved the sad songs. Apparently, people get a little happier singing about someone else's miseries. Legend has it that *Down in the Valley* was composed by E.V. Body while incarcerated in the Birmingham jail. Sing it sad.

Blue

Chorus	Down in the val - ley val- ley so low. Hang your head
	Hear the wind blow dear hear the wind blow. Hang your head

O - ver hear the wind blow.
O - ver hear the wind blow.

Violets love sunshine, roses love dew,
Angels in Heaven know I love you,
Know I love you, dear, know I love you,
Angels in Heaven know I love you.

If you don't love me, then love who you please
Throw your arms 'round me and give my heart ease,
Give my heart ease, dear, give my heart ease
Throw your arms 'round me and give my heart ease.

Throw your arms 'round me before it's too late,
Throw your arms 'round me and feel my heart break
Feel my heart break, dear, feel my heart break,
Throw your arms 'round me and feel my heart break.

Write me a letter, send it by mail
Back it and stamp it to the Birmingham jail,
Birmingham jail, love, Birmingham jail
Back it and stamp it to the Birmingham jail.

Build me a castle a hundred foot high,
So I can see him as he goes by,
As he goes by, dear, as he goes by
So I can see him as he goes by.

Goober Peas

oober Peas dates back to the Civil War when Confederate soldiers, deprived of everything else, still had their humor. Goober peas were nothing but regular old-fashioned peanuts, and Georgia soldiers were fondly known as 'goober grabbers.' Unlike the thousands of songs that were written during the Civil War by professional tunesmiths, *Goober Peas* was one of a handful written by the troops themselves. The words were playfully attributed to "A. Pindar, Esq." and the words to "P. Nutt, Esq."

When a horseman passes, the soldiers have a rule
To cry out at their loudest, "Mister Here's Your Mule"
But another pleasure enchantinger than these
Is wearing out your grinders, eating goober peas!

Just before the battle, the General hears a row
He says, "The Yanks are coming, I hear their rifles now"
He turns around in wonder and what do you think he sees?
The Georgia Militia-eating goober peas!

I think my song has lasted almost long enough
The subject's interesting but rhymes are mighty rough
I wish this war was over, when free from rags and fleas
We'd kiss our wives and sweethearts and gobble goober peas!

17

Grandfather's Clock

Early in the Civil War a poorly clad young man by the name of Henry Clark Work timidly approached the song publishing firm of Root and Cady in the hopes of getting his songs published. Not expecting much, publisher George Root quickly realized that the solemn looking young man sitting before him was a truly gifted songwriter. Root's hunch proved correct. Work's songs were some of the most popular and enduring songs of the nineteenth century. His classics include *Kingdom Coming, Marching Through Georgia,* and *The Ship That Never Returned.* Work composed *Grandfather's Clock* in 1876.

Grandfather's Clock

(continued)

Photo by Wayne Erbsen

In watching its pendulum swing to and fro,
Many hours had he spent when a boy;
And in childhood and manhood the clock seemed to know
And to share both his grief and his joy.
For it struck twenty-four when he entered at the door,
With a blooming and beautiful bride.

My grandfather said that of those he could hire,
Not a servant so faithful he found;
For it wasted no time and had but one desire
At the close of each week to be wound.
And it kept in its place not a frown upon his face,
And its hands never hung by its side.

It rang an alarm in the dead of the night
An alarm that for years had been dumb;
And we knew that his spirit was pluming for flight,
That his hour of departure had come.
Still the clock kept the time, with a soft and muffled chime,
As we silently stood by his side.

Two old timers were nodding off in their chairs at the nursing home. Their wives thought they'd play a little trick on them so they streaked by buck naked in front of the dozing men. Opening one eye, the first old timer said, "Henry, did you see what I just saw?" "I'm not quite sure," replied Henry, "but whatever it was sure needed ironing." [3]

19

Ground Hog

S ometimes they call them "whistle pigs" or "woodchucks." But after they lunch on your garden you'll probably call them a pest! Your revenge can be to invite your friendly Ground Hog to be the guest of honor for supper.

Shoul-der up your gun and whis-tle up your dogs. Shoul-der up your gun and whis-tle up your dogs. We're off to the woods for to catch a ground hog. Ground hog.

Here comes granny walking on a cane (2X)
Says she's gonna eat that ground hog's brain,
Ground hog

Here comes Sal with a great long pole (2X)
Twist that whistle pig outta his hole,
Ground hog

Here comes Sal with a snigger and a grin (2X)
Ground hog grease all over her chin,
Ground hog

I dug down but I didn't dig deep (2X)
There lay a whistle pig fast asleep,
Ground hog

Run here, mama, and run here quick (2X)
This groundhog has made me sick,
Ground hog

I cut a long pole for to twist him out (2X)
Great God a'mighty, what a ground hog snout
Ground hog

> One day I went to see a friend on his farm. He showed me about the place. We came to the pigpen. There was the strangest looking pig I had ever seen. It had a wooden peg-leg!
> We went to the house and my curiosity got the best of me; I asked about the unusual pig.
> One night that pig woke us up, busting down the door, squealing. The house was on fire. He saved our lives.
> "Another time," he continued, "my tractor overturned, pinning me to the ground. Nobody was around; I thought I was a goner. Well, here come that pig running. He grunted and pushed till he got that tractor off me."
> "Amazing," I exclaimed. "But why the wooden leg?"
> "Hell man! You don't eat a great pig like that all at one time!" [4]

Ground Hog

(continued)

You eat up the meat and you save the hide (2X)
Makes the best shoe strings you ever tied,
Ground hog

Children all around, they screamed and cried (2X)
They love ground hog both stewed and fried,
Ground hog

I skinned him, I washed him, I put him on to boil (2X)
I thought, by golly, I could smell him half a moile
Ground hog

Little piece of cornbread laying on the shelf (2X)
If you want any more you can sing it yourself,
Ground hog

In case your gourmet cookbook doesn't include morsel of Ground Hog, here is an actual recipe compliments of Mrs. Gladys Carpenter of Buckeye, West Virginia. Whatever you do, don't throw away the skin. The finest of the old mountain banjos always use a Ground Hog hide for the drum of the banjo.

HOW TO COOK A GROUNDHOG

Take one skinned groundhog with entrails removed. Try to get a young or middle-aged hog. Your old groundhog will be tough. Cut it up and remove the "strong bone" which is under the front armpits. For old groundhogs, soak in strong salt water for about one hour, with one teaspoon of vinegar added. Rinse in fresh water. Boil for 15 or 20 minutes in water with 1 tsp. baking soda added. Rinse and boil for 10 minutes more.

For young groundhogs, eliminate the baking soda step. Now, take your flour and cornmeal of equal proportions, along with salt and pepper, and mix together in a paper bag. Add the groundhog and shake it good so the ingredients even up on it. Then fry it at low speed and prick it with a fork. When the fork penetrates easily, turn it up to high speed and brown. Dash on a little Worcestershire sauce. Serve with cornbread and vegetables.

Hambone

This song uses the oldest musical instrument known to man—the human body. Hambone involves slapping your hands, sides, thighs, mouth and even the top of your head in a rhythmic manner. Ouch!!! It goes back to the very roots of Black music, which was early African drumming. During slavery days drums were treasured as being among the few instruments that were available. However, a slave insurrection in 1739 made drums outlawed because they were thought to communicate imminent revolt. Slaves substituted their own bodies for the outlawed drums, and the results were called "Patting Juba," or Hambone. This version is a variation of the British nursery song *Hush Little Baby, Don't Say a Word* and was collected from Frank A. Hall.

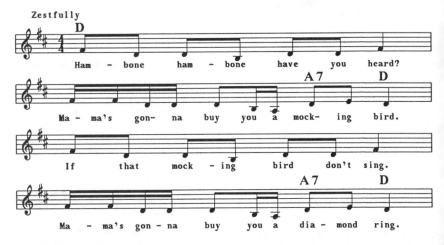

Zestfully

Ham - bone ham - bone have you heard?

Ma - ma's gon - na buy you a mock- ing bird.

If that mock - ing bird don't sing.

Ma - ma's gon - na buy you a dia - mond ring.

If that diamond ring don't shine,
Mama's gonna buy you a bottle of wine.
If that bottle of wine gets broke,
Mama's gonna buy you a billygoat.

If that billygoat don't stay,
Mama's gonna buy you a Chevrolet.
If that Chevrolet don't run,
Mama's gonna buy you a B.B. gun.

If that B.B. gun don't shoot
Mama's gonna buy you a brand new boot.
If that brand new boot don't fit,
Mama's gonna say, "Goodnight I quit."

I was walking down a country road one time when I saw a man struggling to hold a pig up in a tree. Not wanting to appear nosey, I went on by without saying a word. Later that day I came back down the road and there was the same man still struggling to hold that pig up to a tree.
"My dear man," I said. "Isn't that a dreadful waste of time!" The man replied, "What's time to a pig? [5]

Home Sweet Home

O f the two men who composed *Home Sweet Home*, one was homeless and the other was known as a "home-wrecker." The story goes that the words to *Home Sweet Home* were composed by John Howard Payne, who was born in New York City, but who migrated to London seeking his fortune as an actor and playwright. He composed *Home Sweet Home* for the opera "Clari" or "The Maid of Milan." It was first produced on May 8, 1823. Payne's success was mixed with financial failures, and he once served time in a debtor's prison. Eventually, President Tyler awarded Payne the post of American consul at Tunis in 1842. Payne always lamented the fact that he had never had a home.

The melody of *Home Sweet Home* was written by Sir Henry Rowley Bishop, who was an English conductor and composer. Because he had used his melody in an earlier opera, it was assumed that he had pirated it, but Sir Henry successfully defended his claim to authorship in court. Even though *Home Sweet Home* went on to world-wide notoriety, Sir Henry himself was described as "a noted reprobate, home-wrecker and spendthrift; and he died in poverty."

I Was Born About Four Thousand Years Ago

Bragging was not invented yesterday. In fact, people like Davy Crockett made a career out of it: "I can walk like an ox, run like a fox, swim like an eel, yell like an Indian, fight like the devil, spout like an earthquake, make love like a mad bull, and swallow a man whole without choking if you butter his head and pin his ears back." Crockett also modestly claimed to be "half-horse, half-alligator, a little touched with snapping turtle..." Davy Crockett himself would be envious of the exploits of the unknown composer of this famous minstrel song.

Chorus: I was born a-bout four thou-sand years a-go. There ain't no-thin' in this world that I don't know. I seen King Phar-aoh's daugh-ter fish-in' Mo-ses from the wat-er. I can lick the man what says that it ain't so.

I was there when Satan looked the garden o'er,
I seen Eve an' Adam comin' out of the door,
In the bushes I was peepin' at the apple they was eatin',
I can prove that I'm the man what ate the core!

I taught Solomon his little A-B-C's
I showed Noah how to make Limburger cheese
I was sailin' down the bay with Methuselah one day,
And I saved his long white whiskers from the fleas.

I remember when the country had a king
I seen Cleopatra pawn her weddin' ring,
I played ring-around-a-roses with Abednego and Moses,
And I'll fight the man what says that I can't sing!

Two liars got to bragging, and one said he'd been ocean fishing and caught a 500 pound fish.

The second one said he too, had been fishing. He thought he had caught a fish, but it turned out to be a lantern from the Titanic, and he said it was still lit!

The first one pondered this story for a minute and said, "I'll take 200 pounds off that fish I caught if you blow out the lantern." [6]

Jack of Diamonds

When the world began there was one song. Eventually that song got lonely and split in two. Those two songs decided to have babies, and more songs were born, all related to that first song. It's no wonder so many songs sound alike; they're all kin to each other!

Astute music historians have been able to trace *Jack of Diamonds* to a number of close kinfolk including *Rye Whiskey, The Rebel Soldier, Clinch Mountain, My Horses Ain't Hungry,* and *If the River Was Whiskey.* More distant relatives have even been tracked down to the lines of a 1734 London play: "He eats when he's hungry, and drinks when he's dry/ And down, when he's weary, contented does lie."

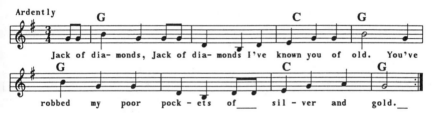

Jack of dia- monds, Jack of dia- monds I've known you of old. You've robbed my poor pock-ets of___ sil-ver and gold.__

Whiskey, you villain,
You've been my downfall,
You've kicked me, you've cuffed me,
But I love you for all

They say I drink whiskey,
My money's my own,
And them that don't like it
Can leave me alone

I'll eat when I'm hungry
I'll drink when I'm dry,
And when I get thirsty
I'll lay down and die

If the ocean was whiskey
And I was a duck,
I'd dive to the bottom
And never come up

Whiskey, rye whiskey,
Rye whiskey I cry,
If I don't get my whiskey
I surely will die

It's beefsteak when I'm hungry
Rye whiskey when I'm dry,
The greenbacks when I'm hard up
And heaven when I die

Be good to your friends. Without them you'd be a total stranger.[7]

Jesse James

When the South lost the War Between the States, some Confederate soldiers kept fighting. Among those who sought to "even the score" was Frank and Jesse James from Clay County, Missouri. Over a fifteen year period beginning in 1868, they held up 12 banks, 7 trains, and 5 stagecoaches in 11 states and territories. Wanted posters were plastered all over the mid-west offering a $5,000 reward, dead or alive.

Although it seemed like every sheriff, posse and pinkerton were after the James gang, Jesse himself was becoming a folk hero, "robbing the rich and giving to the poor." When he was gunned down in his home by Frank Ford, a trusted member of his gang, his death was wildly mourned with newspaper headlines reading "Goodbye Jesse!" This song was composed shortly after his death by Billy Garshade, from the Crack Neck section of Clay County, Mo. and remains the most famous outlaw song.

Stoicly

Jes - se James was a lad who killed man-y a man. He robbed the Glen - dale train._____ He stole from the rich and he gave to the poor. He'd a hand, a heart, and a brain.____

Chorus

Poor Jes - se had a wife to mourn for his life, two chil-dren they were brave.____ But that dir-ty lit-tle coward that shot Mis-ter How-ard Has laid poor Jes-se in his grave.____

Jesse James

(continued)

Library of Congress

A drunk stumbled out of the local tavern and decided he'd take the short cut home, so he cut across the cemetery. It was dark, and he stumbled into a freshly dug grave. He couldn't get out so he started yelling at the top of his lungs.

Finally another drunk from the tavern heard him, walked cautiously to the edge of the grave and looked own. "What's the matter?" he said.

The first drunk said, "Lordy, mister, you got to help me. I'm about to freeze to death down here!"

"Why, no wonder!" the second drunk said. "You ain't got no dirt on you." [8]

It was on a Wednesday night the moon was shining bright
They robbed the Glendale train
The people they did say for many miles away
It was robbed by Frank and Jesse James

It was Robert Ford that dirty little coward
I wonder how he does feel
For he ate of Jesse's bread and he slept in Jesse's bed
Then he laid poor Jesse in his grave

It was on a Saturday night, poor Jesse was at home
Talking to his family brave
Robert Ford came along like a thief in the night
And he laid poor Jesse in his grave

The people held their breath when they heard of Jesse's death
And wondered how he ever came to die
It was one of the gang called Little Robert Ford
He shot poor Jesse on the sly

This song was made by Billy Gashade
Just as soon as the news did arrive
He said there was no man with the law in his hand
That could take Jesse James when alive.

John Henry

John Henry ranks right up there with our finest mythical characters like Paul Bunyan, Santa Claus and the tooth fairy. It is a classic American ballad that pits man against machine. The ballad is based on an actual contest between John Henry and a steam-powered drill at the Big Bend Tunnel in West Virginia about 1870-72. John Henry beat the steam drill fair and square, but his valiant efforts cost him his life.

From Fiddlin' John Carson.

John Hen- ry he was a lit- tle bit- ty boy. He was
sit – tin' on his ma – ma's knee. He
picked up a ham- mer and a lit – tle piece of steel, Lord
ham- mer – 'll___ be the death of me, Lord
ham – mer – 'll___ be the death of me.

John Henry went upon the mountain
Come down on the other side
The mountain was so tall, John Henry was so small
Lord, he lay down his hammer and he cried,"Oh, Lord"
He lay down his hammer and he cried

John Henry was on the right hand
But that steam drill was on the left
"Before your steam drill beats me down
Hammer my fool self to death
Lord, I'll hammer my fool self to death"

John Henry

(continued)

Courtesy of Jim Bollman Collection

John Henry told his Captain
"Captain you go to town,
Bring me back a twelve-pound hammer
And I'll whup your steam drill down
And I'll whup your steam drill down"

For the man that invented that steam drill
Thought he was mighty fine
John Henry drove fourteen feet
The steam drill only made nine
The steam drill only made nine

John Henry told his shaker
"Shaker, you better pray
For if I miss this six-foot steel
Tomorrow'll be your buryin' day
Tomorrow'll be your buryin' day"

John Henry told his little woman
"I'm sick and I want to go to bed
Fix me a place to lie down
Got a rollin' in my head
Got a rollin' in my head"

John Henry had a lovely little woman
Her name was Polly Ann
John Henry got sick and he had to go bed
But Polly drove steel like a man
Polly drove steel like a man

A rural woman went into town to see if she could get a loan to build a bathroom in her house. She had never been in a bank, so she was nervous. She got right to the point with the bank president. "I want to borrow a thousand dollars to put a bathroom in my house."

The president was cautious and responded, "I don't believe I know you. Where have you done your business before?"

"Oh, out back in the pine thicket," she replied. [9]

Listen to the Mockingbird

They called him Whistling Dick, but his real name was Dick Milburn. The year was 1854 and sometimes he ran errands for Septimus Winner's music store in Philadelphia. Other times Whistling Dick could be found on the street begging for pennies and nickels with his guitar and bird whistle imitations. Dick was particularly good at imitating the sounds of a mockingbird, and it was this sound that inspired the twenty-seven year old Septimus Winner to compose *Listen to the Mockingbird*.

The song was published the following year, but slow sales led Winner to sell the copyright for just $5.00. Of course, selling a song that cheap just about guarantees its success. By the end of the century it had sold nearly twenty million copies at home and abroad and was a favorite of both Abraham Lincoln and King Edward VII.

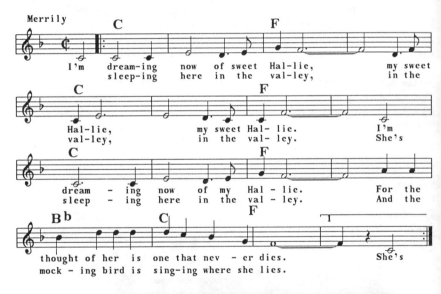

Merrily

C   F

I'm dream-ing now of sweet Hal-lie, my sweet
sleep-ing here in the val-ley, in the

C   F

Hal-lie, my sweet Hal- lie. I'm
val-ley, in the val- ley. She's

C   F

dream - ing now of my Hal - lie. For the
sleep - ing here in the val - ley. And the

Bb   C   F

thought of her is one that nev - er dies. She's
mock - ing bird is sing-ing where she lies.

Listen to the Mockingbird

(continued)

Chorus

Lis-ten to the mock-ing bird, lis-ten to the mock-ing bird.

The mock-ing bird still sing-ing o'er her grave.

Lis-ten to the mock-ing bird, lis-ten to the mock-ing bird.

Still sing-ing where the weep-ing wil-lows wave._

A blacksmith was shaping red-hot horseshoes on his anvil and throwing them down on the ground to cool. A local boy wandered up, reached down, and picked up one of the half-cooled shoes. He quickly dropped it. The blacksmith asked slyly, "Was it hot?" "No, it just don't take me long to look at a horseshoe." [10]

Ah well I yet can remember, I remember, I remember
Ah well I yet can remember
When we gathered in the cotton side by side
'Twas in the mild mid-September
'Twas in the mild mid-September
And the mockingbird was singing far and wide

When charms of spring are awaken, are awaken, are awaken
When charms of spring are awaken
And the mockingbird is singing on the bough
I feel like one so forsaken, so forsaken, so forsaken
I feel like one so forsaken
Since my Hallie is no longer with me now

Moonshiner

Moonshiner is the classic song about a favorite mountain beverage. The first three verses were collected from Currence Hammons, Roscoe Holcolm and Carl Sandburg. The author composed the last two verses. *Moonshiner* is always sung unaccompanied.

Verses 3 & 4 © 1993 by Wayne Erbsen

Tipsy

I've been a moon-shin-er for sev'n-teen long years. I've spent all my mon-ey on whis-key and beers. I'll go to some hol-ler I'll put up my still. I'll make you one gal-lon for a two dol-lar bill.

The revenue officers came by this house in the mountains and asked a small boy where his daddy was. "Making whiskey," the boy said.
"Where?"
"I'll show you for ten dollars," the boy said.
"Ok, let's go."
"Pay me first."
"No, we'll pay you when we get back," the revenuer said.
"You ain't coming back," the boy retorted. [11]

I'll go to some grocery and drink with my friends,
No women to follow to see what I spends.
God bless those pretty women, I wish they were mine,
Their breath smells as sweet as the dew on the vine.

I'll eat when I'm hungry and drink when I'm dry.
If moonshine don't kill me, I'll live till I die.
God bless those moonshiners, I wish they were mine,
Their breath smells as sweet as the good old moonshine.

I been o'er this country, I've been to New York.
I drank all their whiskey, almost swallowed the cork.
Yes I drank all their whiskey, and I slept in their beds.
I've drunk enough whiskey to kill four men dead.

I've sung on this song all the law will allow.
It should have been over long before now.
Yes, my throat is all dried out so I'll take me a glass.
It won't be my first drink, and it won't be my last.

My Home's Across the Smoky Mountains

O ften sung as *My Home's Across the Blue Ridge Mountains,* this song was first collected as *My Own True Love* in 1909 by Louis Land Bascom. The first recording was made by Bascom Lamar Lunsford in the 'thirties.

Forlornly G ... D

Chorus My home's a-cross the Smo-ky Moun-tains. My home's a-cross the Smo-ky

G

Moun - tains. My home's a- cross the Smo- ky Moun - tains. And I

D G

nev - ver ex - pect to see you an - y - more._____

How can I keep from crying
How can I keep from crying
How can I keep from crying
For I never expect to see you anymore

Rock and feed my baby candy
Rock and feed my baby candy
Rock and feed my baby candy
For I never expect to see you anymore

Goodbye my little darling
Goodbye my little darling
Goodbye my little darling
For I never expect to see you anymore

A man was taking tests in a hospital. A nurse asked him to bring a specimen to her in a bottle. He was shy, however, and he talked his wife into returning the bottle to the nurse. "Is this urine?" the nurse asked. "No, it's his'n." [12]

My Old Kentucky Home

My Old Kentucky Home was inspired by Steven Foster's first trip to the South when he paid a visit to the Kentucky mansion of some of his relatives in February of 1852. The sight of slaves toiling in the fields by day and of singing on cabin steps in the evening kindled images that would later appear in numerous songs penned by Foster, including My Old Kentucky Home.

Although he was the son of Northern slave owners, Steven Foster more truly captured the spirit of the Old South in his melodies and lyrics than any tunesmith of his day. Becoming an instant success as first performed by the Ed Christy Minstrels in 1853, My Old Kentucky Home earned Foster the tidy sum of almost $1,400 and the honor of having the official state song of Kentucky.

My Old Kentucky Home

(continued)

Photo by Wayne Erbsen

They hunt no more for the 'possum and the coon
On meadow, the hill and the shore
They sing no more by the glimmer of the moon
On bench by that old cabin door

The day goes by like a shadow o'er the heart
With sorrows where all was delight
The time has come when the darkies have to part
Then my old Kentucky home, good night

The head must bow and the back will have to bend
Wherever the worker may go
A few more days and the troubles all will end
In the field where sugar-canes may grow

A few more days for to tote the weary load
No matter, 'twill never be light
A few more days till we totter on the road
Then my old Kentucky home, good night

Question: What is big at the bottom, little at the top, and has ears!
Answer: A mountain. "But what about the ears!" "Didn't you ever
hear of mountaineers!" [13]

New River Train

The New River, thought to be one of the oldest rivers in the world, cuts a large swath through parts of North Carolina, Virginia and West Virginia. The song was commonly sung around Grayson County, in Southwest Virginia by 1895 and was first recorded by Henry Whitter from nearby Fries, Virginia in about December 1923. There is no end to the verses you can make up to *New River Train*. The final verse is my own contribution to the song.

Chorus I'm riding on that New River Train. Riding on that New River Train. The same old train that brought me here. And it's soon gonna carry me away.

Darling, you can't love one (X2)
You can't love one and have any fun
Darling you can't love one

Darling, you can't love two (2X)
You can't love two and still be true
Darling you can't love two

Darling, you can't love three (2X)
You can't love three and still love me
Darling you can't love three

Darling you can't love four (2X)
You can't love four and love me anymore
Darling you can't love four

Darling you can't love five (2X)
You can't love five and get honey from my beehive
Darling you can't love five

Darling you can't love six (2X)
You can't love six, that kind of love don't mix
Darling you can't love six

Darling you can't love many (2X)
You can't love many or you won't get any
Darling you can't love many

Uncle Dave Macon

A roudy drunk stumbled up to Uncle Dave Macon and inquired, "Where in the Hell have I seen you before!" Uncle Dave replied, "I don't know, brother. What part of Hell are you from!" [14]

Oh! Susanna

Charles Schultz, creator of the Peanuts cartoon strip, once said that every baby ought to be issued a banjo. I would add that along with the banjo and a Teddy bear, a few choice Stephen Foster songs should gently be placed in every baby's crib. *Oh! Susanna* is perhaps Stephen Foster's best known song but few people can sing more than just one verse and the chorus. It was copyrighted February 25, 1848 just in time to be a favorite of the 'forty-niners seeking gold in California.

I come from Al-a-bam-a with my ban-jo on my knee. And I'm goin' to Lou-si-an-a, my true love for to see. It rained all night the day I left, the weath-er it was dry. The sun so hot I froze to death, Su-san-a don't you cry. Oh! Su-san-a Oh, don't you cry for me. For I come from Al-a-bam-a with my ban-jo on my knee.

I had a dream the other night, when everything was still
I thought I saw Susanna, a-coming down the hill.
The buckwheat cake was in her mouth, a tear was in her eye
Says I, I'm coming from the South, Susanna don't you cry.

I soon will be in New Orleans, and then I'll look around
And when I find Susanna, I'll fall upon the ground.
But if I do not find her, then I will surely die
And when I'm dead and buried, Susanna don't you cry.

Oh, Them Golden Slippers

The minstrel craze that swept the country starting in the mid-1840's attempted to portray life on Southern plantations. But absent on the minstrel stage were genuine black minstrels. Instead, white musicians in black-face filled the stage with rollicking renditions of minstrel songs played on banjos, fiddles, tambourines and bones.

Eventually black minstrel troops did appear, including a group calling themselves the Original Georgia Minstrels. Among their ranks was the talented and college educated James A. Bland, who composed many of the classics from the minstrel period including *Oh, Them Golden Slippers* (1879), *Hand Me Down My Walking Cane,* and *Carry Me Back to Old Virginny.* The later was chosen the official state song of Virginia in 1940. Take a deep breath to sing this one. Very deep.

Oh, Them Golden Slippers

(continued)

Oh, my old banjo hangs on the wall,
'Cause it ain't been tuned since way last fall,
But the old folks say we will have a good time,
When we ride up in the chariot in the morning.
There's old Brother Ben and Sister Luce,
They will telegraph the news to Uncle 'Bacco Juice,
What a great camp meeting there will be that day,
When we ride up in the chariot in the morning.

Goodbye children, I will have to go,
Where the rain don't fall or the wind don't blow.
And your ulster coats, why you will not need
When you ride up in the chariot in the morning.
But the golden slippers must be neat and clean,
And your age must be just sweet sixteen,
And your white kid gloves you will have to wear,
When you ride up in the chariot in the morning.

Courtesy of Jim Bollman Collection

A man went to a restaurant, intending to order some brain for supper. The menu read: Fiddle player brain...$2.00/oz.; Mandolin player brain...$3.00/oz; Guitar player brain...$4.00/oz; Banjo player brain...$100.00/oz. Complaining, the man asked the waiter, "Why is banjo player brain so expensive?" "Do you know how many banjo players it takes to get one ounce of brain?" [15]

Old Dan Tucker

Old Dan Tucker, the comic song about a good-for-nothing ne'er-do-well, was written by Dan Emmett around 1830-31, before he was seventeen years old. Emmett apparently based the song on the life of a mischievous rascal he knew who was always getting into some kind of trouble.

In 1842, Emmett and several of his musical cronies decided to audition their new minstrel sound in front of an enthusiastic if inebriated crowd in the Bowery district of New York City. Calling themselves the "Virginia Minstrels," the first song they sang was *Old Dan Tucker*. To their unanimous surprise, the sound was a 'hit,' and so began the minstrel craze, which was to sweep the nation from the Broadway stage to the gold fields of California to the riverboats on the Mississippi River.

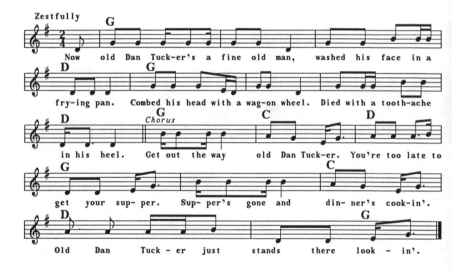

Now old Dan Tuck-er's a fine old man, washed his face in a frying pan. Combed his head with a wag-on wheel. Died with a tooth-ache in his heel. *Chorus* Get out the way old Dan Tuck-er. You're too late to get your sup-per. Sup-per's gone and din-ner's cook-in'. Old Dan Tuck-er just stands there look-in'.

Old Dan Tucker came to town
Riding a billygoat and leading a hound
Hound dog barked and the billy goat jumped
Throwed old Dan Tucker right straddle of a stump

I come to town the other night
To hear the noise and see the fight
The watchman was a running around
Crying old Dan Tucker's a come to town

How do you tell if a banjo player is sitting in a level spot?

❧ *The tobacco juice runs out of both sides of his mouth.* [16]

Old Joe Clark

Although no one has yet admitted being the originial Old Joe Clark, the song paints a picture of a crusty old timer who was always into some kind of tomfoolery. It ranks right up there with *Turkey in the Straw* and *Soldier's Joy* as the best known of all Southern tunes, and there is scarcely a fiddler who can't saw out a rendition of it. The song seems to invite creating new verses about the escapades of Old Joe Clark, and variants run into the hundreds. This text was collected by folklorist Artus Moser who, at this writing, is 98 years young. Bill Monroe, known as the father of Bluegrass music, remembers going far out into the field and practicing his singing on songs like *Old Joe Clark.*

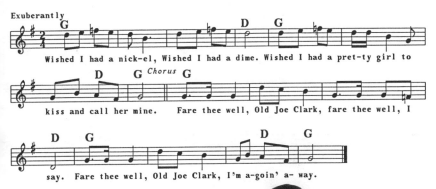

Wished I had a nick-el, Wished I had a dime. Wished I had a pret-ty girl to kiss and call her mine. Fare thee well, Old Joe Clark, fare thee well, I say. Fare thee well, Old Joe Clark, I'm a-goin' a-way.

I will not marry an old maid
I'll tell you the reason why.
Her neck is so long and stringy
I'm afraid she'll never die.

I asked my girl to marry me
And what do you think she said.
Time enough to marry you
When all the rest are dead.

Old Joe Clark did take sick
And what do you think ailed him.
He drank a churn of buttermilk
And then his stomach failed him.

Old Joe Clark did get drunk
And not a word could he utter.
He fell down on the supper table
And stove his nose in the butter.

On Top of Old Smoky

The setting of "Old Smoky" is the Smoky Mountains of Western North Carolina, named for the smoky haze that hangs over it, especially in early mornings. The verses freely "float" between *Rye Whiskey, I'm Troubled, Rabble Soldier, Texas Cowboy, My Horses Ain't Hungry, The Cuckoo,* and *The Inconstant Lover.* This version was collected as *The Wagoner's Lad* by the English folk song collector Cecil Sharp on July 29, 1916 from Miss Memory Shelton at Allegheny, NC. Sharp and others were convinced the song originated in England. The most popular version these days is *On Top of Spaghetti.*

Sparking is pleasure,
Parting is grief,
And a false-hearted lover
Is worse than a thief

A thief will but rob you,
Will take what you have,
And a false-hearted lover
Will take you to the grave

The grave will decay you,
Will turn you to dust
There is not one girl out of a hundred
A poor boy can trust

They will tell you they love you
To give your heart ease,
And as soon as you back up on them
They'll court who they please

It's a-raining and a-hailing,
The moon give it no light
Your horses can't travel
This dark, lonesome night

Go put up your horses,
Feed them some hay,
Come sit down here by me
As long as you stay

My horses are not hungry,
Won't eat your hay,
So farewell, my little darling,
I'll feed on my way

I will drive on to Georgia,
Write you my mind
My mind is to marry, love
And leave you behind

Polly Wolly Doodle

Even as a kid I was fascinated by the crazy words of *Polly Wolly Doodle*. Considered one of America's classic "nonsense" songs, it was a favorite of the minstrel stage in the 1850's. Its first known printing was in *Student's Songs* published June 9, 1880 by Harvard students.

Frolicsome

D
Oh, I went down South for to see my Sal. Sing-ing

A7
Pol- ly wol- ly doo- dle all the day.__ My__ Sal she is a

D Chorus
spun - ky gal, sing-ing Pol- ly wol-ly doo-dle all the day.__ Fare the

A7
well, fare the well, fare the well my fai - ry fay. For I'm

goin' to Lou - si - an - a, for to see my Su- sy- ann-a, sing-ing

D
Pol - ly wol - ly doo - dle all the day.

Oh, my Sal, she is a maiden fair,
Singing Polly wolly doodle all the day,
With curly eyes and laughing hair,
Sing Polly wolly doodle all the day.

I came to the river and couldn't get across,
Sing Polly wolly doodle all the day,
I jumped on a donkey and thought he was a hoss,
Sing Polly wolly doodle all the day.

A grasshopper sitting on a railroad track,
Sing Polly wolly doodle all the day,
A picking his teeth with a carpet tack,
Sing Polly wolly doodle all the day.

What's the difference between the Prince of Wales, a papa gorilla, and a bald head?

☛ The first is an heir apparent, the second is a hairy parent, the third has no hair apparent. [17]

Poor Ellen Smith

They say that *Poor Ellen Smith* was written by convicted murderer Peter de Graff while awaiting execution by the electric chair in 1893. Be careful when you sing it in Forsyth County, North Carolina...you might get arrested. Tempers were running so hot about the trial, that a law was passed making it a misdemeanor to sing *Poor Ellen Smith* in a gathering of any size because it always fomented a riot. The melody was pilfered from the hymn *How Firm a Foundation*.

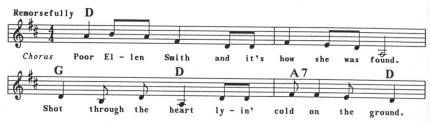

Chorus: Poor El-len Smith and it's how she was found. Shot through the heart ly-in' cold on the ground.

Saw her on Monday before that sad day
They found her poor body and took her away

Well I went away to Winston, I prayed all the time
The man might be found that committed the crime

The sheriff and blood hounds they struck on my trail
Over the mountains and down through the fields

They picked up their Winchesters hunting me down
But I'd gone away to that Mount Airy town

Now that they have me, I know I must die
The truth to you I'll tell, since I never will die

"Mrs. Morton, dear me, how do you do! How's your husband!"
"Oh! He's in a very bad state."
"My gracious! I never heard he was sick. And what kind of a state is he in!"
"Why he's in the state prison." [18]

Photo by Wayne Erbsen

Poor Wayfaring Stranger

Poor *Wayfaring Stranger* is a Southern Appalachian religious folk song that has been passed down by the hands of singers from both the white and black traditions since the time of the American Revolution. The melody bears some resemblance to several of the older ballads such as *Come All You Fair And Tender Ladies*. The earliest known version of *Poor Wayfaring Stranger* appeared in print under the title *Judgement* in Ananias Davisson's *Kentucky Harmony* published in 1816. It was later printed in the *Sacred Harp* hymn book in 1844.

Woebegone

I'm just a poor way-far-ing stran-ger. A trav-ling through this world of woe. But there's no sick-ness, toil, or dan-ger. In this bright world to which I go. I'm go-ing there to see my fath-er. I'm go-ing there no more to roam. I'm just a go-ing o-ver Jor-dan. I'm just a go-ing o-ver home.

I know dark clouds will gather round me
I know my way is rough and steep
Yet beauteous fields lie just before me
Where God's redeemed their vigils keep

   I'm going there to see my mother
   She said she'd meet me when I come
   I'm only going over Jordan
   I'm only going over home

I'll soon be freed from every trial
My body sleeps in the church-yard
I'll drop the cross of self-denial
And enter on my great reward

   I'm going there to see my Savior
   To sing His praise forevermore
   I'm only going over Jordan
   I'm only going over home

Pretty Polly

Pretty Polly is based on an actual murder by John Billson, a ship's carpenter, near Gosport, England. The wicked deed was captured in a ballad published in about 1727 as *The Gosport Tragedy* and sung to the tune *Peggy's Gone Over Sea*. It tells the chilling tale of the murder of his pregnant lover and the flight aboard the ship M.M.S. Bedford. The story takes a haunting turn when the seaman Charles Stewart was confronted in the dark hold of the ship by a ghost with a baby in her arms. When questioned by Captain Edmund Hook, the real villain saw the ghost of his lover before him, fell to his knees, and confessed to the grisly crime. He subsequently died aboard the ship, presumably of scurvy.

Spooky / G

Oh,__ Pol- ly, pret-ty Pol- ly, come go a-long with me._____

Pol- ly, pret-ty Pol- ly, come go a- long with me._____ Be-

D / G

fore we get mar - ried some plea - sure to see._____

Oh Willie, Oh Willie I'm afraid of your ways (2X)
I'm afraid you're a-leading my body astray

Pretty Polly, Pretty Polly you guess about right (2X)
For I dug on your grave the most part of last night

He led her over the hollow through the valley so deep (2X)
At last Pretty Polly began to mourn and weep

Let's go a few steps further and we'll see what we can spy (2X)
A new dug grave and a spade lying by

He stabbed it to her heart, the blood began to flow (2X)
Into the grave Pretty Polly did go

He threw the dirt over her and started for home (2X)
Leaving no one to weep but the wild birds to mourn

A debt to the devil Willie will have to pay (2X)
For killing Pretty Polly and running away

Julius was sent to the apothecary shop for some dye, but he forgot the name of it. He asked the clerk: "What do folks dye with?"

"Why the cholera, sometimes," said the clerk.

"Yes, I believe that's the name of it," said Julius. "Give me 5 cents worth." [19]

Railroad Bill

His real name was Morris Slater, but they all called him Railroad Bill. To authorities, he was an outlaw who robbed trains by throwing selected items out boxcar doors, to be retrieved later. To folks in rural Alabama in 1894, he was a folk hero who took from the rich and gave to the poor. Bill was so good at outrunning the law, that legends tell of him turning into different animals to avoid capture. Some claimed it would take a silver bullet to kill him.

This version of Railroad Bill recorded by Riley Pickett and Gid Tanner, September 11, 1924.

Brazenly

D

Rail-road Bill___ migh-ty bad man.___ Shot the lan- tern from a

G   D   A   D

brake man's hand. Well it's ride,___ ride,___ ride.___

Some folks say a dummy can't run
Just let me tell you what the dummy done

Left Atlanta half past one
Got to Chattanooga at the setting of the sun

Railroad Bill lives on the hill
He wouldn't work, Lord and he never will

Kill the chicken, send me the head
You think I'm a-working, I'm at home in the bed

Baby, baby don't you fret
I ain't no fool about you yet

Kill the chicken, send me the wing
Think I'm a-working, well I ain't doin' a thing

Kill me a chicken, send me its feet
Think I'm a-working, I'm a-walkin the street

This lady and her baby were heading west on a train. The conductor came through collecting tickets, spotted the baby, and said, "Lady, that's the ugliest baby I've ever seen." The lady burst into tears. A gentleman sitting nearby brought over a glass of water to console her and said, "and here's a banana for your monkey." [20]

The Riddle Song

Most old time folk songs are fickle. They can't seem to make up their minds and so the words often change with every singing, and the verses drift aimlessly from song to song, searching for just the right place to be.

The Riddle Song, which is sometimes called *I Gave My Love a Cherry*, is a rare exception. It has remained virtually unchanged through countless singings since it first descended from the ancient English ballad *Captain Wedderburn's Courtship*. Perhaps it was perfect to start with. But whatever the reason, it has led an exciting life, traveling west with Daniel Boone's followers from Kentucky in covered wagons and becoming a favorite of frontier children.

Serenely

F   Bb   F

I gave my love a cher-ry that has no stone. I

C   F   C

gave my love a chick-en that has no____ bone. I

F   C

gave my love a ring____ that has no end. I

Bb   F

gave my love a ba - by____ with no cry - in'.

How can there be a cherry that has no stones?
How can there be a chicken that has no bones?
How can there be a ring that has no end?
How can there be a baby that's not cryin'

A cherry when it's blooming it has no stones,
A chicken when its pipping it has no bones,
A ring when it's rolling it has no end,
A baby when it's sleeping there's no cryin'

> *Cure for the gout: Live on sixpence a day, and earn it.* [21]

Roving Gambler

A gambling man who caught the fancy of a young lady tended to be a mother's and father's worst nightmare. Well-dressed with a gold watch bob adorning a silk vest, he cut a dashing figure and wooed many an unsuspecting damsel away from loving parents. *The Roving Gambler* is based on an 18th century British broadside ballad and has been variously called *The Guerrilla Man, The Roving Journeyman,* and *The Gamboling Man.* It was known in the Ozarks as early as 1875.

Slothfully

I am a rov-ing gam-bler, I've gam-bled all a-round. When ev-er I meet with a deck of cards, I lay my mon-ey down. Lay my mon-ey down, lay my mon-ey down.

I've gambled down in Washington
I've gambled over in Spain
I'm going down to Georgia
To gamble my last game

I had not been in Washington
Many more weeks than three
'Til I fell in love with a pretty little girl
And she fell in love with me

She took me to her parlor
She cooled me with her fan
Whispered low in her mother's ear
I love this gamblin' man

Mother, Oh dear Mother
You know I love you well
But the love I have for the gambling man
No human tongue can tell

Daughter, Oh dear daughter
How can you treat me so
Leave your dear old mother
And with the gambler go

Mother, Oh dear Mother
I'll tell you if I can
If you ever see me coming back
I'll be with the gambling man

A man walked into a bar with his alligator and asked the bartender, "Do you serve banjo players here?"
"Sure do," replied the bartender.
"Good," said the man. "Give me a beer and I'll have a banjo picker for my 'gator." [22]

Soldier's Joy

Soldier's Joy is the most well-known of all the fiddle tunes. Some say it's a descendant from an English tune called *The Kings Head*. In the South it used to be called *Payday in the Army* or *Love Somebody*.

I am my ma-ma's dar-ling boy. I am my ma-ma's dar-ling boy. I am my ma-ma's dar-ling boy. Sing a lit-tle song called Sol-dier's Joy.

Grasshopper sitting on a sweet potato vine
Grasshopper sitting on a sweet potato vine
Grasshopper sitting on a sweet potato vine
Along come a chicken and says, "You're mine!"

Fifteen cents for the morphine
Twenty-five cents for the beer
Fifteen cents for the morphine
They're gonna take me away from here

I'm gonna get a drink, don't you want to go
I'm gonna get a drink, don't you want to go
I'm gonna get a drink, don't you want to go
All for the soldier's joy

I love somebody, yes I do
I love somebody, yes I do
I love somebody, yes I do
And I bet you five dollars, you can't guess who

Wayne Erbsen

A group of people were sitting around at the wake of a man who died the unusual death of drowning in a barrel of whiskey mash at the still he was operating. His wife was wringing her hands and carrying on in a pitiful way.

"I wouldn't take it too hard, ma'am," her husband's fellow moonshiner said. "I think he died happy. He got out and went to the bathroom three times before he died." [23]

The Sunny South

The *Sunny South* probably dates from the 1850's, with some sources crediting it only to "Raymond." It was first recorded by Charlie Poole and the North Carolina Ramblers in May of 1929. This verson comes from Allan's *Lone Star Ballads*, 1874.

Chorus: Take me home to the place where I first saw the light. To the sweet sun-ny South take me home. Where the mock-ing birds sing me to rest ev-'ry night. Oh why was I tempt-ed to roam.

I think with regret of the dear ones I left,
Of the warm hearts that sheltered me there
Of the wife and dear ones of whom I'm bereft
And I sigh for the old place at home

Take me home to the place where the orange trees grow,
To my cot in the evergreen shade,
Where the flowers on the river's green margin may blow
Their sweets on the banks where we played

The path to our cottage they say has grown green,
And the place is quite lonely around
And I know that the smiles and the forms I have seen,
Now lie deep in the dark, mossy ground

Take me home! let me see what is left that I know
Can it be that the old home is gone!
The dear friends of my childhood indeed must be few
And I must lament all alone!

But yet I'll return to the place of my birth
Where my children have played at the door,
Where they pulled the white blossoms that garnished the earth,
Which will echo their footsteps no more

A man came home late rather intoxicated, with a jar of moonshine in his hand. His wife was waiting at the door for him. She grabbed the jar and said, "I'm going to see what there is in this stuff that you like so much." She took two or three big swallows, lost her breath, coughed, turned red, and sputtered, "This stuff is terrible!"

Her husband gazed her into focus and said, "And all this time, I'll bet you thought I was enjoying it." [24]

Turkey in the Straw

Carl Sandburg said it best: *Turkey in the Straw* smells of hay thrown "over barn dance floors, steps around like an apple-faced farmhand, has the whiff of a river breeze when the catfish are biting, and rolls along like a good wagon slicked up with new axle grease on all four wheels."

Even though *Turkey in the Straw* is as American as "Corn on the Cob," almost a dozen Scottish, Irish and English tunes claim the honor of inspiring it. When first published in 1834 as *Old Zip Coon*, both George W. Dixon and the team of Bob Farrel and George Nickols swore they wrote it. In 1861 Dan Emmett nicely added to the confusion by publishing a new song called *Turkey in the Straw*. Emmett's title quickly attached itself to the melody of *Old Zip Coon* and black-faced minstrels had a field day making up new verses which by now could fill up a good-sized barn.

Turkey in the Straw

(continued)

Oh, I went out to milk but I didn't know how
I milked a goat instead of a cow
A monkey sittin' on a pile of straw
A-winkin at his mother-in-law

Then I come to the river and I couldn't get across
So I paid five dollars for an old blind horse
Well he wouldn't go ahead, and he wouldn't stand still
So he went up and down like an old saw mill

I met Mr. Catfish comin' down stream,
Says Mr. Catfish, "What does you mean?"
Caught Mr. Catfish by the snout
And turned Mr. Catfish wrong side out

As I came down the new cut road
Met Mr. Bullfrog, met Miss Toad
And every time Miss Toad would sing
Ole Bullfrog cut a pigeon wing

Courtesy of Jim Bollman Collection

A man got a flat tire and he pulled over next to an insane asylum. One of the inmates looked through the bars and noticed the man's predicament: he had lost all the lug nuts off that one wheel. The man was desperate, and sat down on the curb to cry.

The inmate shouted, "Mister, why not borrow one lug nut from the other three wheels?"

The man was overjoyed and inquired why such a brilliant man was thus incarcerated in an asylum.

"I may be crazy, but I'm not stupid." [25]

Uncle Joe

Uncle Joe started out its long life as a Scottish piper's tune known as *Miss McCleod's Reel.* It then made the perilous journey to America aboard a crowded ship and eventually found itself in the South being played by fiddlers at local dances. It was first spotted in Putnam County, Georgia in 1856 and published in Joel Chandler Harris' *Uncle Remus.*

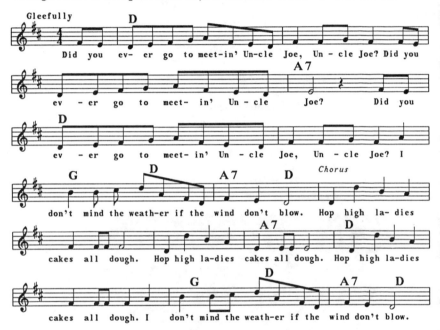

Will your horse carry double Uncle Joe, Uncle Joe
Will your horse carry double Uncle Joe
Will your horse carry double Uncle Joe, Uncle Joe
I don't mind the weather if the wind don't blow

How's your rheumatism Uncle Joe, Uncle Joe
How's your rheumatism Uncle Joe
How's your rheumatism Uncle Joe, Uncle Joe
I don't mind the weather if the wind don't blow

Is your horse a single footer Uncle Joe, Uncle Joe
Is your foot a single footer, Uncle Joe
Is your horse a single footer Uncle Joe, Uncle Joe
I don't mind the weather if the wind don't blow

The Unclouded Day

The Unclouded Day, by Rev. J.K. Alwood, was first recorded in the early 'twenties by Homer A. Rodeheaver, who was the songleader for the evangelist Billy Sunday. It was also a hit in the 'twenties by Smith's Sacred Singers, in the 'thirties by Cliff Carlisle, and in the 'seventies by Willie Nelson.

Oh, they tell me of a home far be-yond the skies. Oh they tell me of a home far a-way. Oh they tell me of a home where no storm-clouds rise. Oh they tell me of an un-cloud-ed day. Oh, the land of cloud-less day. Oh, the land of an un-cloud-ed day.

Oh they tell me of a home where my friends have gone
Oh they tell me of that land far away
Where the tree of life in eternal bloom
Sheds its fragrance through the unclouded day

Oh they tell me of a King in His beauty there
And they tell me of that land far away
Where the tree of life in eternal bloom
In the city that is made of gold

Oh they tell me that He smiles on His children there
And His smile drives their sorrows all away
And they tell me that no tears ever come again
In that lovely land of unclouded day

Wabash Cannonball

Alan Lomax best described the mythical train known as the Wabash Cannonball: "Each tie was made from an entire redwood tree. The conductor punched each ticket by shooting holes through it with a .45 calibre automatic. The train went so fast that after it was brought to a dead stop, it was still making sixty-five miles an hour." The song was first printed in 1904 but was based on an earlier song by the name of *The Great Rock Island Route!* by J.A. Roff, published in 1882.

Reprinted from Ozark Folksongs by Vance Randolph, by permission of the University of Missouri Press. Copyright by the Curators of the University of Missouri.

Jovially

G

From the great At - lan - tic oc - ean to the
Chorus Lis - ten to the jin - gle, the

C   **D**

wide Pa - ci - fic shore. From the queen of flow-ing moun-tains, to the
rum - ble and the roar. As she glides a-long the wood-land, through

G

south bells by the shore. She's migh- ty tall and hand-some and
hills and by the shore. Hear the migh- ty rush of the en-gine. Hear that

C   **D**   **G**

quite well known by all. She's the com-bin-a-tion of the Wa-bash Can-non-ball.
lone-some ho - bo squall. Trav-lin thru the jun-gle on the Wa-bash Can-non-ball

She come down from Birmingham one cold December day,
And she rolled into the station you could hear the people say,
There's a girl from Birmingham, she's long and she is tall,
She come down to Birmingham on the Wabash Cannonball.

Here's to Daddy Claxton, may his name forever stand,
And always be remembered in the courts of Alabam,
His earth race is over and the curtains 'round him fall,
We'll carry him home to victory on the Wabash Cannonball.

When Johnny Comes Marching Home

Despite bitter differences, the North and the South did share one thing during the Civil War—music. Home folks on both sides of the conflict rejoiced in singing *When Johnny Comes Marching Home*. Written in 1863 by Patrick S. Gilmore, the song became a national hit not only during the Civil War but later in the Spanish American War.

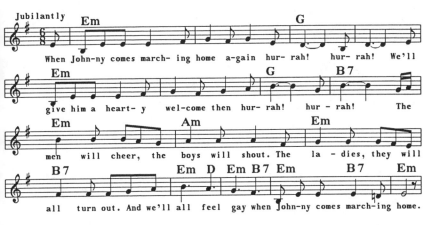

When John-ny comes march- ing home a-gain hur- rah! hur- rah! We'll give him a heart- y wel-come then hur- rah! hur - rah! The men will cheer, the boys will shout. The la - dies, they will all turn out. And we'll all feel gay when John-ny comes march-ing home.

The old church bell will peal with joy,
Hurrah, hurrah!
To welcome home our darling boy,
Hurray, hurray!
The village lads and lassies say
With roses they will strew the way,
And we'll all feel gay when
Johnny comes marching home

Get ready for the jubilee,
Hurrah, hurrah!
We'll give the hero three times three,
Hurrah, hurrah!
The laurel wreath is ready now
To place upon his loyal brow,
And we'll all feel gay when
Johnny comes marching home

Let love and friendship on that day,
Hurrah, hurrah!
Their choicest treasures then display,
Hurray, hurrah!
And let each one perform some part,
To fill with joy the warrior's heart,
And we'll all feel gay when
Johnny comes marching home

When You And I Were Young, Maggie

Lest we forget, *Maggie* was written as a poem by Canadian George W. Johnson, who was a scholar and poet. He wrote the poem about his student and sweetheart Maggie Clark, and about the old mill where they used to meet. Johnson published the poem himself in a collection named *Maple Leaves*. The poem caught the eye of the English composer/conductor James Austin Butterfield who set the words to music while living in Chicago. The real Maggie and George Johnson were married in 1865, but alas, she died that same year before knowing that the song about her would be published the following year and become a classic.

When You And I Were Young, Maggie

(continued)

Wayne Erbsen & Barbara Swell

Photo by Martin Fox

A man stopped at a hotel where I work. After he dismounted and tied his horse, he said to the landlord, "Can I get lodging here tonight?"

"No," said the boss. "Every room in the house is engaged."

"Well, can't you even give me a blanket and a bunch of shavings for a pillow in your barroom?"

"No sir, there's not a square foot of room anywhere in the house."

"Well then," said the traveler, "I'll thank you to shove a pole out the second floor window and I'll just roost on that." [26]

A city so silent and lone, Maggie
Where young and gay and best
In polished white mansions of stone, Maggie
Where they each found a place for their rest

Is built where the birds used to play, Maggie
And join in songs that were sung
We sang just as gay as did they, Maggie
When you and I were young

They say I am feeble with age, Maggie
My steps less sprightly than then
My face is a well-written page, Maggie
Then but time, time alone was the pen

They say we are aged and gray, Maggie
As spray by white breakers flung
To me you're as fair as you were, Maggie
When you and I were young

Whoa Mule

I f you've ever tried courting in a mule-driven sleigh, you can identify with *Whoa Mule*. It was first recorded by Riley Puckett in 1924. This version comes from Tom Ashley.

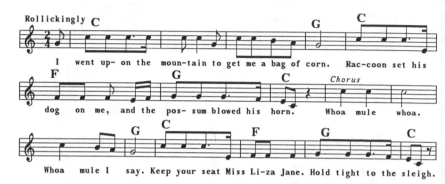

Rollickingly

I went up- on the moun-tain to get me a bag of corn. Rac-coon set his dog on me, and the pos- sum blowed his horn. Whoa mule whoa. Whoa mule I say. Keep your seat Miss Li-za Jane. Hold tight to the sleigh.

Whoa mule, whoa
Whoa mule I holler
Tie a knot in that mule's tail
And he'll go through the collar

Went up on the mountain,
Give my horn a blow
Thought I heard some pretty girl say
Yonder comes my beau

I would not marry a tall, slim gal,
Tell you the reason why
Her neck's so long and stringy
I'm afraid she'd never die

I went to kiss my gal last night
I thought I would do it sneakin'
I missed her mouth and hit her nose
And the doggone thing was leakin'

A peanut sittin' on a railroad track
His heart was all a-flutter
Around the curve come a passenger train,
Toot toot peanut butter!

Wes Erbsen

Photo by Wayne Erbsen

Wild Bill Jones

The ballad of *Wild Bill Jones* is the South's equivalent to the famous shoot-out at the OK Corral. Although historians are loth to track down the original Wild Bill, the ornery cuss left this song as a trail for us to follow from North Carolina to Mississippi to Arkansas. The last verse can be sung as a chorus.

As I walked out for to take a lit – tle walk. I
He was walkin' and a talk- in' by my true lov – er's side. I

walked up – on that Wild Bill Jones.____
bid him to leave her alone.____

He said my age is twenty-one,
Too old for to be controlled
So I drew my revolver from my side
And I destroyed that poor boy's soul

So it's pass around that long-neck bottle
And we'll all go out on a spree
For today was the last of that Wild Bill Jones
And tomorrow'll be the last of me

He reeled and he staggered and he fell to the ground
And he gave one dying groan
I threw my arms around my darling's neck
Saying baby won't you please come home

They sent me to prison for twenty long years
This poor boy longs to be free
But Wild Bill Jones and that long-necked bottle
Has made a ruin of me

Courtesy of Jim Bollman Collection

> *I had a fellow working for me on the sawmill one time and he got too close to the saw and cut his ear off. It fell down into the sawdust pit and he was down looking for it. When I came by, I said, "What are you doing down there?" He said, "I cut my ear off and I'm looking for it!" I said, "Well, I'll help ya!" I got down and found the ear. I said, "Here it is!" He took it and looked at it carefully. Directly he said, "Keep looking; mine had a pencil behind it!"* [27]

Wildwood Flower

I like to call *The Wildwood Flower* "The Hillbilly National Anthem," because it's one of the all-time favorite guitar pieces. It became a country classic after being recorded by the Carter Family for Victor records in the l930's. The song was first published in 1860 by Maud Irving and J.P. Webster. Little is known about Maud, but J.P.'s real name was Joseph P. Webster. He was an active melodist during the Civil War and wrote the tunes to such classics as *Lorena* and *Sweet By and By.*

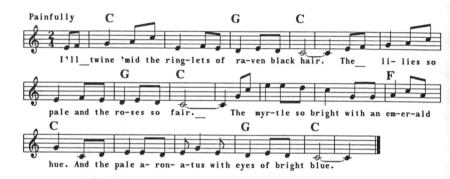

I'll sing and I'll dance, my laugh shall be gay
I'll cease this wild weeping, drive sorrow away;
Tho' my heart is now breaking, he never shall know
That his name made me tremble and my pale cheek to glow

I'll think of him never, I'll be wildly gay,
I'll charm every heart and the crowd I will sway;
I'll live yet to see him, regret the dark hour
When he won then neglected the frail wildwood flower

He told me he loved me, and promised to love
Through ill and misfortune, all other above
Another has won him, oh! misery to tell
He left me in silence, no words of farewell!

He taught me to love him, he call'd me his flower
That blossom'd for him all the brighter each hour
But I woke from my dreaming, my idol was clay
My visions of love have all faded away

A teacher was having trouble teaching arithmetic to one little boy. So she said, "If you reached in your right pocket and found a nickel, and you reached in your left pocket and found another one, what would you have?"

"Somebody else's pants," said the little boy. [28]

Yellow Rose of Texas

hen it was first published in 1858, all that was known about *The Yellow Rose of Texas* was that its composer identified himself only as "J.K." Since then, dogged research has raised the possibility that the mysterious J.K. was Joseph Kelp, who arranged "Aura Lee" for publication in 1864. The Yellow Rose herself was a mulatto indentured servant named Emily D. West who played an important part in the history of Texas independence. It was Emily who kept the Mexican General Santa Anna busy while American troops slipped up on and defeated the Mexican army in a siege known as the Battle of San Jacinto.

There's a yel-low rose of Tex-as that I am goin' to see. No oth-er sol-dier knows her no sol-dier, on-ly me. She cried so when I left her, it like to broke my heart. And if I ev-er find her we nev-er more will part.

Where the Rio Grande is flowing and the starry skies are bright
She walks along the river in the quiet summer night
She thinks if I remember, when we parted long ago,
I promised to come back again, and not to leave her so

Oh! now I'm going to find her, for my heart is full of woe,
And we'll sing the song together, that we sung so long ago
We'll play the banjo gaily, and we'll sing the songs of yore,
And the yellow rose of Texas shall be mine for evermore

> *This boy was out plowing a mule that was bad to kick, and a neighbor came along and said, "Son, I know that mule is bad to kick. Has he ever kicked you?"*
> *"No, sir," he said, "but several times he's kicked right where I've been."* [29]

Courtesy of Jim Bollman Collection

Index of Songs

Sources for Jokes: [1] Author's collection [2] Darrell Reich [3] Author's collection [4] Bill Reed, *Laughter in Appalachia* [5] Author's collection [6] Margaret Rader, *Hometown Humor, USA* [7] David Holt [8] Billy Edd Wheeler, *Laughter in Appalachia* [9] Becky Nelson, *Laughter in Appalachia* [10] Jack Marema, *Curing The Cross-Eyed Mule* [11] Jim Ralston, *Curing The Cross-Eyed Mule* [12] Dan Greene, *Curing The Cross-Eyed Mule* [13] Author's collection [14] Author's collection [15] Darrell Reich [16] Fred Park [17] Author's collection [18, 19] *New Book of Black Wit, 1856* [20] Author's collection [21] *New Book of Black Wit, 1856* [22] Darrell Reich [23] Glen Baker, *Laughter in Appalachia* [24] Loyal Jones, *Hometown Humor, USA* [25] Author's collection [26] *New Book of Black Wit, 1856* [27] Glen Baker, *Laughter in Appalachia* [28] Loyal Jones, *Hometown Humor, USA* [29] Bob Hannah, *Hometown Humor, USA*